FLORENCE
a journey of dreams

Photography by
H. SIMEONE HUBER

Texts by
GLORIA FOSSI

Translation by
GILES WATSON

MAGNUS

Florence - Pride of the Chroniclers of the Past.

Florence possesses the seven most important – indeed, the only – things a city should possess. So said an enterprising and adventurous Florentine, Benedetto Dei, at the end of the fourteenth century. Dei had travelled extensively in his capacity as a Florentine diplomat, merchant and, above all, as a messenger for the Medicis, the lords of Florence. He had been to Africa, Asia and every country in Europe and swore, with understandable pride, that he had never seen a city to compare with his own.

What were these seven qualities which Florence possessed? After all, Florence was a city without a "broad, extensive territory" as the historiographer and artist, Giorgio Vasari, was to write later, in the mid-sixteenth century. The city lies wedged between the surrounding hills and the river Arno.

First and foremost, Benedetto Dei wrote, Florence enjoyed "complete liberty". Then, the city had a "large population of rich, well-dressed citizens". Third, there was the "torrent" of fresh water which crosses the city, that is to say the Arno, not to mention its many mills. In fourth place, Florence had "dominion over cities and castles and lands and peoples". Fifth, there was the "Studium" (the university) with its "Greek and calculus" and sixth, "every craft complete and perfect". Finally, there were branches of Florence's banks in every corner of the globe.

The Florence best-known today is the Renaissance Florence of austere palazzos and courtyards with statues, fountains and tiny gardens but by the fourteenth century, as the chroniclers of the time report, Florence was already the most beautiful, the richest and the most important city in the known world, boasting paved streets, lofty towers and public buildings and loggias as well as great churches. Fifteenth-century Florentines were also able to affirm proudly that their city was the most beautiful, the richest and the most important and, indeed, by then, it was the city with the largest number of artists in Italy. Florentines of the past, rather like their present-day descendants, were proud, conceited and parochial but what they had to say about their immediate surrounding environment was and is difficult to deny. How, then, did such a high concentration of master craftsmen, important buildings and wealth come about?

History from the Hills.

Let us make a journey back in time over the history of Florence and its monuments as historical events intertwine with the vicissitudes of the leading figures in the city's public and cultural life. Let us first take a look at the city from the hills. From Bellosguardo hill, from Piazzale Michelangelo, Forte del Belvedere, Fiesole or Settignano, we cannot avoid the imposing form of Brunelleschi's dome, "raised above the skies", as the architect, Leon Battista Alberti, commented in the mid-fifteenth century. However, even before the dome covered the vast complex of the cathedral of Santa Maria del Fiore, Florence must have had a character which set it apart from other cities.

From one point of view, medieval Florence could be considered a smaller version of modern Manhattan, with towers taking the place of skyscrapers. Today, very few of those ancient towers remain. They can be seen in Borgo Sant'Jacopo, just over the Arno, not far from the Ponte Vecchio bridge, or in Por San Maria, not far from the ancient St. Mary Gate, which is no longer extant. The towers were usually solid, square constructions but one round tower, the so-called Pagliazza tower, still stands in a little square near Via delle Oche. Today, it is the Hotel Brunelleschi. This tower, like so many other less well-known medieval Florentine buildings, was erected over the remains of a building dating from the days of the Roman Empire for Florence has a history which goes much further back in time and almost all of which lies buried underground.

Ancient Roman Roots.

This is beautiful Florence, or rather, *Florentia,* as its citizens once called it to remind the world that it was a city in bloom with a wealth of flowers. According to an ancient legend, the little Roman colony which grew up in the first century BC or thereabouts was founded in spring during the festival of the *Ludi floreales.* Medieval Florence spread out from the small core formed by the Roman city, which centred on what is now Piazza della Repubblica, the ancient Forum. Ancient *Florentia* was considered by medieval and Renaissance chroniclers, somewhat mistakenly, to be a "little Rome" and had its own Capitoline temple, the "Capitol", commemorated up until the end of the last century in the name of a small church built in the early Middle Ages, Santa Maria al Campidoglio.

Like every Roman town, *Florentia* had its thermal baths and also a large theatre on the edge of what is now Piazza della Signoria, in the area of Via dei Gondi and Via dei Leoni. There was an amphitheatre whose perimeter can still be traced in the twists and turns of some of the streets leading to Piazza Santa Croce and there must also have been temples, as even Dante mentions them in a somewhat ambiguous manner. In the *Divine Comedy,* the poet mentions a temple dedicated to Mars on the site of the Battistero, "fine St. John's", but this is almost certainly incorrect. The Battistero is built on the remains of a large edifice dating from the first century AD but which was, in all likelihood, private rather than public. Dante's mistake, perhaps committed deliberately, is repeated by a fourteenth-century chronicler, Giovanni Villani and also by humanists such as Coluccio Salutati and Leonard Bruni, both men of letters active in the political life of the Florentine republic, in the fourteenth and fifteenth centuries. The "mistake" is explained by the fact that, until the disastrous flood of 1333, an equestrian statue believed to be of the god Mars stood at the head of the Ponte Vecchio bridge over the Arno. The statue was said to have stood previously on the top of a column inside the temple, supposed to have been dedicated to Mars, on whose foundations the Battistero was to rise.

Legends always exist for a reason and this one clearly derives from the desire on the part of the Florentines in the late Middle Ages and Renaissance to make the city's rather obscure, humble origins seem as much like Rome's as possible. There was, of course, at Rome, a famous equestrian statue, that of Marcus Aurelius, on a column in the Lateran square.

It is not easy to estimate the importance of the original city but the town plan of Roman *Florentia* can still be made out as one looks down on the city. The layout, that of a Roman *castrum,* was quadrilateral, crossed by two intersecting main streets, the *cardo maximus,* comprising the present-day Via Roma, Via Calimala and Via Por Santa Maria, and the *decumanus maximus,* now Via Strozzi, Via degli Speziali and Via del Corso.

Excavations of ancient Florence continue to bring to light important remains, thanks to the efforts of archaeologists. In particular, the finds demonstrate that the city was built and rebuilt many times in layers as new buildings replaced older ones.

The City of Towers.

In the Dark Ages and Middle Ages, Florence was a jungle of massive, towering buildings which looked very different from today's city and was intimately linked to a past so remote that not even the Florentines of the Renaissance were able to comprehend it in full. A few centuries later on, there was only a faint echo of medieval Florence, the crowded life of its narrow streets and the noise in the shadow of its towers left. The only open spaces in the Middle Ages were provided by the occasional markets and the courtyards of the churches. Until the fifteenth century, there were only modest buildings and no dome by Brunelleschi towering over everything. There was only one great light-filled facade, in a classical style like its ancient marble, that of San Miniato al Monte and this, as the name suggests, was up on the hill. Down in the city, there was only one great building, the Battistero, whose origins are still the subject of debate.

The rest of the town comprised wooden houses and menacing stone towers with few windows, as tightly closed and suspicious as their occupants. The towers were barricaded in narrow streets and were sometimes intercommunicating, thanks to galleries, corbels and bridges. It was possible to go from one room to the one above by using a rope ladder which could be drawn up should an enemy attack, and enemies were always near at hand. Doors were therefore mere slits and houses were veritable fortresses.

This, then, was medieval Florence, the Florence of continuous rebuilding. How can we best imagine it to have been?

Naturally, we need to make an effort, but it is well worthwhile. Let us look at the Florence of today from the hills. As we have already mentioned, wherever we choose to look from, whether it be Fiesole or Bellosguardo or Forte Belvedere, the view of the city is dominated by Brunelleschi's dome and yet, even when we have managed, regretfully, to

eliminate its perfect shape from the view in our mind's eye, bell-towers pop up like mushrooms all around to remind us of an older past which also expressed itself vertically. Those bell-towers serve to point out a feature which exists no longer but which did exist before Brunelleschi built his dome and that is the ancient Florence of towers. It was the Florence of Dante's noble ancestor, Cacciaguida, the Florence which, as Dante himself nostalgically lamented, "had no empty family houses". Dante did not mean houses that were "empty" in the sense of having the luxury of space to spare or abandoned in the fierce struggles between Guelphs and Ghibellines. He meant "empty" as a result of the many violent deaths of his day.

Dark, disease-ridden Florence.

In the twelfth century, before the Franciscan monks arrived, the area where the church of Santa Croce was to stand was marshy and insalubrious. The Dominican church of Santa Maria Novella on the other side of the town from the church of Santa Croce was "among the vines" and, for this reason, there still exists a street called Via della Vigna Nuova (New Vine Street).

Just outside the walls on the other bank of the Arno lay the houses of the ever more populous outlying districts, crowding closer and closer in towards the limited area within the walls in an effort to be nearer the centre. Large carts could not use the city's narrow streets and goods were transported on muleback. To own a shop was a privilege as space was at a premium. What space it was possible to rent out for shops and workshops was exploited to such an extent that even the well-off used every available corner for this purpose. In what is now Via del Proconsolo, around the Badia church, there was a succession of such establishments. Soon after the construction of the second ring of city walls in 1205, temporary buildings on the moat of the earlier ring were turned into shops despite a ban imposed by the city authorities.

It would be out of place to feel nostalgic today for a town which was, by and large, gloomy and unhealthy but the Florentines of the early fourteenth century were themselves sorry to have lost their towers.

"Once upon a time, there was a little town" Lapo da Castiglionchio told his son at that time, "that in a short space of time acquired one hundred and fifty 'citizen's' towers. There were also the towers on the city walls. The private towers were each one hundred and twenty fathoms tall". That is to say, they were seventy metres, or well over two hundred feet, high. By the end of the fourteenth century, the towers had long been reduced to a maximum of fifty fathoms, less than half their previous height. This is the story told by Lapo, who was one of the leading figures on the Guelph side and after the Revolt of the Ciampi, or Wool-carders, on 22nd June, 1378, had been among the first to have to leave Florence in haste. He was also to see his house burnt down by his (Florentine) enemies. Lapo's lament was for the good old days when "with its many tall towers, Florence showed one and all both near and far that it was the finest, most vigorous land on earth on such a small territory".

The order in 1250 to reduce the height of the towers, factional symbols and, indeed, instruments of civil strife, was intended to maintain the peace in a period when the Guelph star was in the ascendant but in fact the measure proved of little practical use. Two years previously, in 1248, the Ghibellines had been victorious and had razed their enemies' towers to the ground. The Guelph towers were torn down, as Giovanni Villani's chronicle recounts, and among these there was a particularly large one which stood at the end of Corso degli Adimari in Piazza San Giovanni. As the dead were buried on this spot – there was a cemetery in the open space –, the Ghibellines cut the tower at its base. They then propped it up in such a way as to "make it fall on the church of St. John when the props were burnt". God, as the chronicler tells us, was pleased to spare the church and the one hundred and twenty-fathom high tower fell into the square.

The Guelphs then returned to dominance and after them the Ghibellines again following the battle of Montaperti in 1260. Once again, palazzos and towers were burnt – 59 towers, 47 palazzos, 198 houses, 9 workshops, 10 tenter-yards and a warehouse. This list has survived because, when the tables turned yet again, the owners of all the above claimed damages from the *Comune* (city authorities).

However, the towers had had their day. Palazzo dei Priori, or Palazzo della Signoria, which was later on to be called Palazzo Vecchio, was built on its present site because of the "tower syndrome". It was to have been constructed where the Uberti tower had stood but, because the Ubertis belonged to the faction which was in disgrace at the time, the palazzo was built a little further on at the corner so that it should not touch the "accursed" ground of the family.

The Palazzos.

We are now in fifteenth-century Florence, a city eager to build, to change the features of the older, "vertical", town of medieval towers and bell-towers. This was a new Florence which gradually emerged from the tangle of twisting alleyways and the jungle of now truncated towers to identify in itself a microcosm, the well-proportioned core beyond improvement which it was the city's boast to represent. It was a Florence of feverish building activity which in little more than a century transformed the face of the city. The Florentines of the day must have been proud and excited. "In the time of Cosimo de' Medici and *messer* Luca Pitti, beautiful *Florentia* made 33 walls" wrote the diplomat, Benedetto Dei.

What exactly were these "walls" of which Dei boasted at the end of the fourteenth century?

The "Walls".

Of all these, pride of place went to "the famous dome of Santa Maria del Fiore" – "with its ball" – the chronicler adds with pride. Benedetto Dei had observed, collected information and performed

diplomatic services for the Medicis from Antwerp to Timbuctoo and had seen nowhere to compare with Florence. It was not just the dome that made the little city famous because there were other "walls", as Benedetto writes in his *Cronica*. There was the great Pitti residence and then those of the Medici, Pazzi and Rucellai families. Others belonged to the Aldobrandinis, the Puccis, the Salviatis, the Spinellis and the Martellis "and a hundred others I shall not retail here" the chronicler adds with his usual pride.

These "walls" were real walls of solid stone, a mark of solidity and wealth. They were walls of "highest fame" and also of "great expense". Dei tells us that there was wealth in those houses, a wealth which had by that time become an empire and had made Florence for over a century the most populous, important and beautiful city in the western world.

How had all this been possible? Some recent theories maintain that the explanation is quite simple and that both the building fever and the wealth and beauty of the private palazzos were the result of a happy combination of circumstances. There was an ideal relationship between the demand of the wealthy, who wished to show off their fortune (and so their power and prestige) and the supply of exceptional entrepreneurial and technical skills among the builders whether they were artists, architects, skilled craftsmen or mere labourers.

The skills had been accumulated over the preceding centuries and the artists and artisans often came from outwith Florence, as they always had. In any case, few of the artists were true Florentines, born in the shadow of the towers within the narrow circle of the medieval walls. Giotto, for example, who was from Mugello, was no Florentine and neither was the great architect of Santa Croce and the Palazzo della Signoria, and first designer of Santa Maria del Fiore, Arnolfo di Cambio, who was from Colle Val d'Elsa. Masaccio was not from Florence either, but from Valdarno. Place of birth was not an important factor, however. Whether the artists were outsiders or local, it was a series of special circumstances which made Florence so different.

A great town plan.

Let us take a further step back in time to understand how and why this was so. We shall take as our starting-point another important date, the year 1284. In that year, Arnolfo, the architect and sculptor "of experience and guile", was called in as a consultant on the plans for the third ring of city walls. The *Comune* was planning the final stage in a revolutionary, systematic town plan, the first real town plan in the modern sense to be drawn up for a medieval city. Florence was transformed in a few, short decades. The first streets along the river were laid out, the "Lungarno" avenues of our day, while new city gates and hospitals were built. Via Larga (the present-day Via Cavour) enhanced the city's elegance reaching the San Gallo gate at the end of the Mugnone river. Conceived as a straight line, the street penetrated the heart of the city from the north and allowed carts to pass with wheat from Mugello. An artificial lake was even planned in the "Prato" area, near the gate of the same name.

It was also laid down that the houses in Piazza San Giovanni should be elegant and avoid colour schemes which clashed with the classical style of the Battistero. The use of "sporti" (corbels) in wood or brickwork was banned, or at least restricted, on the upper floors of houses as they jeopardized both elegance and hygiene as well as making the streets even darker.

The Franciscan and Dominican churches, Santa Croce and Santa Maria Novella, were built at opposite ends of the city. The Augustinians came down from the hills to found the church of Santo Spirito. The Servites arrived and the church of Santa Annunziata grew in importance. There were also the public palazzos, the Bargello, for Councils of the People, and then the Palazzo dei Priori, the future Palazzo della Signoria.

The new city walls had increased the city's total area considerably and the *Comune* had committed huge financial resources to the effort. In 1333, there was disastrous flooding and, in 1348, the plague described in Boccaccio's *Decameron*. However, these crises passed and Florence was finally ready, at the turn of the fifteenth century, for the great palazzos.

The building fever was inspired by a need to entertain and to display, private ends this time which mingled with and contributed to the public image of the city. The Craft Guilds commissioned the shrines of the church of Orsanmichele, which had once been a granary, and promoted competitions for the Battistero doors. Charitable associations had already sponsored loggias, such as the Bigallo loggia on the corner opposite the Battistero, in the fourteenth century. In the following century, Brunelleschi conceived the sublime portico of the Spedale degli Innocenti, where foundlings were given shelter.

The Magnificent Patrons.

The real private citizens were the Medicis, the Rucellais and the Strozzis. Not only did these powerful families boast private chapels decorated by famous artists in the most important churches but they also had palazzos built with painstaking attention to detail by the leading architects of the day. Brunelleschi was commissioned by Cosimo de' Medici to design the palazzo in via Larga (today called Palazzo Medici-Riccardi) but the designs were thrown out as being too sumptuous and *avant-garde*. By the mid-fifteenth century, Cosimo was effectively the ruler of the city and the facade Brunelleschi planned right opposite the church of S. Lorenzo, the Medici church *par excellence,* would have made it rather too obvious to the citizens of Florence just who was in charge.

So it was that Michelozzo, who had been the Medicis' architect for some time, suggested a more prudent solution and a sober facade as massive as a castle's now closes the palazzo off from what is now Via Martelli and was then Via Larga. The internal courtyard, where the Medici "board of directors" entertained its visitors, is austere but still offers clear

symbols of those ideals of liberty and justice so dear to the Florentines in the *David* and *Judith* fashioned by Donatello. Opulence is present but hidden from the eye while power underlies the whole without being obvious.

For this reason, the *Procession of the Magi* with its fairy-tale air painted by Benozzo Gozzoli on the upper floor of the family chapel could only be seen on important occasions by foreign dignitaries who were passing through Florence. These were the people who had to understand – and fear – the nature and wealth of the Medicis. The Magi represent the Medicis themselves while the procession alludes to an event which contributed to the glory of the family, the Ecumenical Council which Cosimo had managed to move many years previously from Ferrara to Florence, a jewel of diplomacy with the Church.

There were palazzos, then, but also loggias, places for meetings and ceremonies. Wonderfully spectacular celebrations were held in both public and private loggias. In the course of the fifteenth century, they became the prestigious Florentine setting for the ceremonies of the most influential families. Let us listen to the account of a great feast the wealthy Giovanni Rucellai organized in his loggia, still called Loggia Rucellai today, for the wedding of his son, Bernardo, to Nannina, daughter of Piero de' Medici.

Giovanni was justly proud as his family was being joined through the marriage to the most powerful family in Florence and one of the most powerful families in the known world. "I became related to Piero, son of Cosimo de' Medici, and to Lorenzo and Giuliano" Rucellai begins in his Lenten commonplace book, "and it is for this reason that I am esteemed, honoured and held in high regard. I enjoy their good fortune and prosperity with them". His family crest could also, at last, intertwine with the emblems of the Medicis, the feathers and the diamonds.

A feast in the Loggia.

The feast went as follows. Outside the palazzo on a high platform placed, as Rucellai tells us, between the loggia and the facade of the palazzo in Via della Vigna, a splendid arrangement of curtains, tapestries, drapes and back-rests was set up, all under a "sky" of turquoise drapes to protect it from the sun. There was a sideboard with wrought silver cutlery and the wedding feast was the most sumptuous that Florence had ever witnessed.

This is what Rucellai tells us and we may well believe him but there were other wonderful feasts held in the loggias, as we know from the splendid decorations on the chests which today can only be found in museums. In Piazza San Giovanni, opposite the Battistero, another wedding feast must have enthralled the Florentines. On a famous painted chest now in the Gallery of the Academy, we see depicted a procession of men and women walking past to the sound of trumpets. The sky is of the turquoise material with yellow lilies which also usually covered the route of processions during the feast of St. John, patron saint of the city.

City of Princes and Astrologers.

When building, the Florentines listened to the Music of the Spheres, the Harmony of the Cosmos and to their astrologers. In the fifteenth and sixteenth centuries, architects and engineers, artists and decorators were no longer enough. After the towers, bell-towers, loggias, churches and the earliest palazzos, building fever began to take on all the characteristics of a pathological condition.

The fever was so high that the noblest – and richest – citizens of Florence seemed to have been struck down by a strange virus, a sort of tarantism or dancing fever. The image is used here quite seriously just as Luca Landucci, a Florentine merchant, was not joking when, speaking in 1489 about the magnificent new Gondi (in Piazza San Firenze) and Strozzi palazzos, he said that the people of Florence were *atarentati* ("had been bitten by tarantulas") such was their mania to build "and for this reason, there was a shortage of building materials and workers".

"Tarantism" led in 1489 to Lorenzo the Magnificent's proposal to the Seigneury of a law which would exempt from all taxation for forty years whoever built new houses. A little later, it was the same Lorenzo the Magnificent who complained to the Pope about the problem of "suitable sites for those who want to build". The lack of building space was so severe that only the Pope could help him by ceding to him the last free sites in the city, which all belonged to the Church.

The most serious problem was, however, that of guaranteeing Eternity, not for the patrons but for their palazzos. Michelangelo wrote as follows in the sixteenth century – a fine house and only a fine house can give true honour to its occupant. This honour must last and is, indeed, the only honour which can last forever. The body dies but walls remain if, of course, they are massive and solid and if, too, they are attractive to look at and born under the best auspices of the stars.

In this way, there grew up a neo-Platonic need to imitate the harmonious movement of the heavenly bodies, regulated by the music of the spheres. This in turn led to the harmonious proportions of Renaissance palazzos in Florence, with the help of a little astrology and a little superstition.

Let us imagine for a moment a scene from Florence on the Day of Judgement with palazzos destroyed and houses in ruins. The shocked survivors would have at least one consolation (or pointless pastime) in searching for the coins their ancestors used to place in the foundations of their palazzos, for this was another aspect of the Florence of the fifteenth and sixteenth centuries.

The great Filippo Strozzi, as powerful and rich as the Medicis, took a shovel in hand and began personally to cover over the foundations of his palazzo, designed by Giuliano da Maiano. It was he who threw in a commemorative coin, minted especially for the occasion. On the obverse of the coin was an effigy of Filippo himself and on the reverse, his device. He left his mark all over the palazzo, too.

Vanity of vanities, as Bernardo of Chiaravalle would have said in the Middle Ages and in the Florence of Lorenzo the Magnificent, Savonarola said much the same thing. It is in your honour, not God's, thundered the Dominican monk, referring to the luxury and open ostentation of the new palazzos. Times had changed and while Cosimo the Elder, the Grand Old Man of Florence, had thought better of openly flaunting his possessions and power, his son, Piero, gave way to the public glorification of his family. He could thus openly spend 4,000 golden florins (this was a colossal sum) on marble alone for the church of Santa Annunziata. A short time later in the church of San Miniato, he was even able to place his personal device alongside the symbols of the Calimala (or Merchants') Guild, despite an initial ban by the Corporation. Times were changing with a vengeance and old Cosimo's calculated moves, those of a "private citizen" as the historian, Guicciardini, called him, were now being replaced by the figure of a prince.

In Lorenzo's day, famous Florentines preferred to think about ensuring their survival in eternity and calculated the construction schedules of their buildings in accordance with the Order of the Universe and the astrological calendar. Leon Battista Alberti had already posed the question. It was of fundamental importance to establish the right, the most propitious, day for work to begin. So it was that the neo-Platonist, Marsilio Ficino, whose theories probably inspired Botticelli's *Spring,* turned his hand to astrology. He advised Filippo Strozzi to cover the foundations of his palazzo on 6th August – and only on 6th August – 1489 while building was to start exactly two weeks later.

The astrological tradition in Florence had its roots in the remote past. In the Middle Ages, in the so-called "scarsella" or "purse" of the Battistero, a complex astrological system was depicted. In the fifteenth century, a horoscope was painted on the small cupola of the old sacresty of San Lorenzo (it is still there) while Brunelleschi conceived an astronomical instrument for Paolo dal Pozzo Toscanelli, which was placed in the cathedral. The link between building and astrology was indissoluble in sixteenth-century Florence at the time of the Grand duke, Cosimo I.

He restructured and redecorated Palazzo Vecchio before moving in with his wife, Eleonora of Toledo, in 1541. After having been Palazzo dei Priori (Priors' Palace), then Palazzo del Popolo (People's Palace) and Palazzo della Signoria (Palace of the Seigneury), the building finally became the residence of the Prince.

Cosimo had been born in June and had as his ascendant sign of the zodiac Capricorn. This was also the sign of his ancestor, Lorenzo the Magnificent, as it had been of other famous *condottieri,* amongst whom was the emperor Augustus. For this reason, Cosimo had new coins minted bearing the image of Capricorn, as had Augustus. The symbol also often appears in the decoration of the reception rooms in Palazzo Vecchio.

Let us go forward now to 1564, when Cosimo abdicated power in favour of his son, Francesco.

These were the times when the learned prince emerged at night from his private study to ride abroad in his carriage with another extravagant genius, Bernardo Buontalenti, famous for his fireworks and the complicated sets which enchanted spectators at the Medici theatre. Bernardo was known not only for his alchemistic experiments but also for his marvellous Mannerist constructions, such as the sublime marble staircase he designed for Santa Trinita, today in Santo Stefano al Ponte.

The Fortresses.

Florence was now rebuilt and perhaps the time of "tarantula bites" was over but the dangers of seige and war remained. The golden age of the great palazzos was followed by that of the fortresses. The Fortezza da Basso was built and also the Forte di Belvedere, probably designed by Buontalenti at the request of the Grand Duke Ferdinando I for defensive purposes, to maintain order, as a refuge and as a safe for the treasure of the Medicis.

However, the most famous and inspired building, an example of architecture and town planning conceived as a single whole, is the Uffizi. It began life as reception offices but quickly became, on the upper floors, one of the oldest and perhaps most famous museums in the world. Vasari outdid himself with the corridor which goes from the Uffizi to the Lungarno avenues over the Ponte Vecchio bridge to reach the Boboli gardens and Palazzo Pitti, which by this time was a residence of the Grand Duke.

It was thought a matter of no consequence that to build the Uffizi, as had been the case so often in the past, it was necessary to demolish a large number of older buildings. Indeed, the Grand Duchy had begun life with a Prince, Cosimo, who had been unwisely (if only metaphorically) placed by the Council, when he came to power, on a magnificent charger, as Benvenuto Cellini wrote with characteristic sarcasm. "They gave him the reins with complete freedom in a beautiful field of flowers and fruit and many delights. Then they ordered him not to go beyond certain limits. You tell me who might hold him back when he wants to do so? Laws cannot be imposed upon one who is their lord and master." In the case of the Uffizi, however, the sacrifice was worthwhile.

The City of the Grand Dukes.

By the middle of the sixteenth century, the city was complete and had been built, or rather rebuilt, over the course of at least two centuries on top of the foundations of medieval towers, the earliest churches and wooden hovels. The great palazzos both public and private had been erected and from 1565 on, Vasari's corridor provided a spectacular aerial causeway linking the Uffizi to the Grand Ducal residence at Palazzo Pitti. In the Uffizi itself, the revolutionary Tribune designed by Buontalenti for Francesco I was opened in 1584. Brimming with works of art, precious objects and rare curiosities, the Tribune was one of the earliest examples of museum architecture to be illuminated from above by daylight.

Florence was defended by its two great fortresses, the Forte del Belvedere high up in the hills and the other, dedicated to St. John, down in the city, the Fortezza da Basso (Lower Fortress). Florence had a Mint and the ramparts reached the city walls in the area of the present-day Piazza Tasso from the Boboli hills. There were also the San Miniato fortifications to give some guarantee of sturdy defence in those days of constant fear. Michelangelo took part in the construction of these and even today, broad stretches come down by the Porta San Giorgio gate at the edge of the Forte del Belvedere towards the church of San Niccolò. Florence had its cathedral and the great churches restructured by Giorgio Vasari and, in addition, there were the markets. Moreover, there were new loggias, like the one in Mercato Nuovo (the New Market, today known as the "Straw Market"), and new fountains as well as cloisters and refectories with frescoes by the leading artists of the day – Andrea del Sarto, Rosso Fiorentino, the elder Ghirlandaio, Perugino and many others.

In the churches, there were new chapels, some of which, like the chapel of the Annunziata in the church of Santa Felicità on the far side of the Arno a few yards from the Ponte Vecchio bridge, are painted in a highly emphatic style with bold, frigid colours. Evidently, the early decades of the century, decades of religious and political crisis, favoured the creation of extraordinarily intense works of art which lay, on the surface, outwith the Florentine tradition of a classical sense of proportion. The chapel in Santa Felicità belonged to Ludovico Capponi. Pontormo had frescoed it in a bout of feverish activity during the most difficult period of the sixteenth century in Florence, the decade immediately preceding the seige and restoration of the Medicis in 1530.

The Florence of the Medicis was a Florence of symbols. Palazzo Vecchio had by this time been redecorated with a complex iconography which sang the praises of the Medicis, a family of no particularly ancient roots. For precisely this reason, the Medicis needed to enhance their public prestige. They could also afford, thanks to their vast financial empire, to buy alliances with the major ruling houses of Europe. The Emperor Charles V had allowed the Medicis to return in the person of Alessandro de' Medici in 1529 and in 1536, Alessandro had received the title of Duke. His successor, Cosimo, had wisely remained faithful to the Empire and had been amply rewarded for his loyalty. His Spanish wife, Eleonora of Toledo, the beautiful and celebrated Eleonora of Agnolo Bronzino's portraits, was the daughter of the Viceroy of Naples. She brought a breath of luxury to the still somewhat strait-laced Tuscan city and every aspect of Florentine life was affected by the new "courtly" spirit.

In 1565, there came the final touch. Cosimo's son, Francesco I, managed to gain the hand of an Austrian Archduchess in a triumph of diplomacy which meant more feasts, more pomp and yet more symbols.

The Symbols of Power.

There seemed to be no space left in Florence to build anything new but the Medicis still thought something was missing. That is to say, it would have been missing if artists, sculptors and architects had not known how to "fill" it with new signs, the signs of power. It was a power which could not, and should not, have been kept hidden any longer, so let us follow the development of these symbols.

We shall start with a column of pink marble, one of the fixed points along the route of formal processions around the city of the Grand Dukes. It is the column of Justice, in Piazza Santa Trinità, which every formal procession through sixteenth- and seventeenth-century Florence had to pass and every illustrious foreigner's carriage had to visit. The visitor might then continue across the bridge at Santa Trinità towards Via Maggio, and then on to the column of San Felice in its square (no longer extant). From there, our visitor might reach the palazzo that had once belonged to the Pittis and was now the finest of the Medicis' residences. Eleonora of Toledo had bought the palazzo in 1549 from Buonaccorso Pitti. It boasted not just extensive architectural and decorative restructuring and the magnificent courtyard designed by Ammannati, which was later to be the site of a stunning "naumachy" (staged naval battle) after having been filled with water. The real boast of the palazzo was its gardens, the Boboli Gardens, the green lung of a city which had lost so many gardens and vineyards. The Boboli were full of statues, grottoes and fountains and formed a verdant theatre set which was both salubrious, as Leon Battista Alberti had said of city gardens in the fifteenth century, and also the setting for plays and long promenades, all in complete privacy. It was, all in all, a kind of Olympus on earth, a place of privilege, full of allegorical significance for a family which had become almost divine. The gardens were a symbol of the Medicis' power, indeed omnipotence, with obelisks and porphyry pools as the opulent outward signs of a continuing classical tendency at the height of the Mannerist period. From the Boboli gardens, we shall go back to the column in Piazza Santa Trinità. Shall we take the official visitor's route through fifteenth-century Florence? Ideally, we should do so by night, starting from the final destination of the route on the far side of the Arno in Via Maggio and going backwards towards the beginning. On the Santa Trinità bridge, faithfully rebuilt after the war to Ammannati's sixteenth-century design, a spectacular sight awaits us, scenic in the fullest sense of the word. It really does look like a theatre set as we gaze on the palazzos ranged along the Lungarno avenues and the Mannerist facade of the church of Santa Trinità, designed by Buontalenti, all hinging on the column in the square. The perspectives provide unique effects which can be experienced from Borgo Santi Apostoli, from where Via Porta Rossa emerges into the square, from Via delle Terme or face on from Via del Parione. The official route arrived here having passed other corners and other fountains. At the Carnesecchi (Salt Pork Vendors) corner at the junction of Via Rondinelli, Via dei Banchi and Via Cerretani, there was even

Giambologna's famous sculpture of Hercules and the Centaur, later moved to the Loggia dei Lanzi. During feasts, the statue became a Fount of Bacchus and gave forth wine to the passers-by.

Let us go back to Piazza Santa Trinità. Wherever did the tall column we walk past without a second glance on our way into Via Tornabuoni come from? It came, in fact, from the Thermal Baths of Diocletian in Rome. Thus it was important because it was classical and inspired that feeling which from the Middle Ages on strove to ennoble the, in truth, humble origins of Roman *Florentia*. Medieval, and Renaissance, Florence ought to have been, it was felt, and therefore was, a new Rome, in imitation of the most powerful and magnificent city of antiquity.

In the sixteenth century, Florence also looked to Etruria to justify the absolute dominion of the Medici Dukes over the other cities in Tuscany. Cosimo I had to be a modern *magnus dux Aetruriae* (great leader of Etruria) who had not only succeeded in acquiring the title of Grand Duke from Pope Pius IV but had also tried everything, or rather exhausted the ingenuity of his learned subjects, including that of Pier Francesco Giambullari, the canon of San Lorenzo and member of the Academy of Florence, to demonstrate Florence's Etruscan roots. This included the derivation of the "modern" Florentine tongue from "Aramaic-Etruscan" stock, thus establishing a direct link between the ancient kings of Etruria and the new rulers.

Let us go back now to the column of Justice. It arrived in Tuscany from Rome, or rather Ostia, at the Medicis' port of Leghorn (Livorno) and from there reached Florence in solemn pomp. Its purpose was to demonstrate formally the prince's power and it also commemorated the victory of Florence in 1554 over Siena at the battle of Montemarciano. The pink granite column finally had to act as a symbol of another source of pride, the Pope's gift to Cosimo of the title of Grand Duke. Thus it was an official symbol and by no means the only one in the Florence of the Grand Dukes.

Let us now take a stroll to Piazza Signoria, the site *par excellence* for Medici emblems. Every statue and every sculpture in the square symbolizes something, not just the equestrian statue dedicated by Giambologna to Cosimo I – and the base decorated in bas-relief with highlights from Cosimo's political career – but also and above all the Fountain of Neptune by Ammannati. This is the so-called "Biancone" (Great White Statue), a veritable manifesto of the Medicis' naval power, which was based at Leghorn. Our Florentine tour might ideally come to an end in Piazza dell'Annunziata where we find a symbol to end all symbols on the base of the equestrian statue of Fernando I, designed by Pietro Tacca at the beginning of the seventeenth century. This is a swarm of bees milling around the queen bee, a stunning work both in its perspective and its significance. Over it, we find the motto, *Maiestate Tantum* (Much through Majesty), as if to say that the rulers were both fair and feared, thus allowing their subjects to accumulate huge wealth, exactly as the bees do.

Gloria Fossi

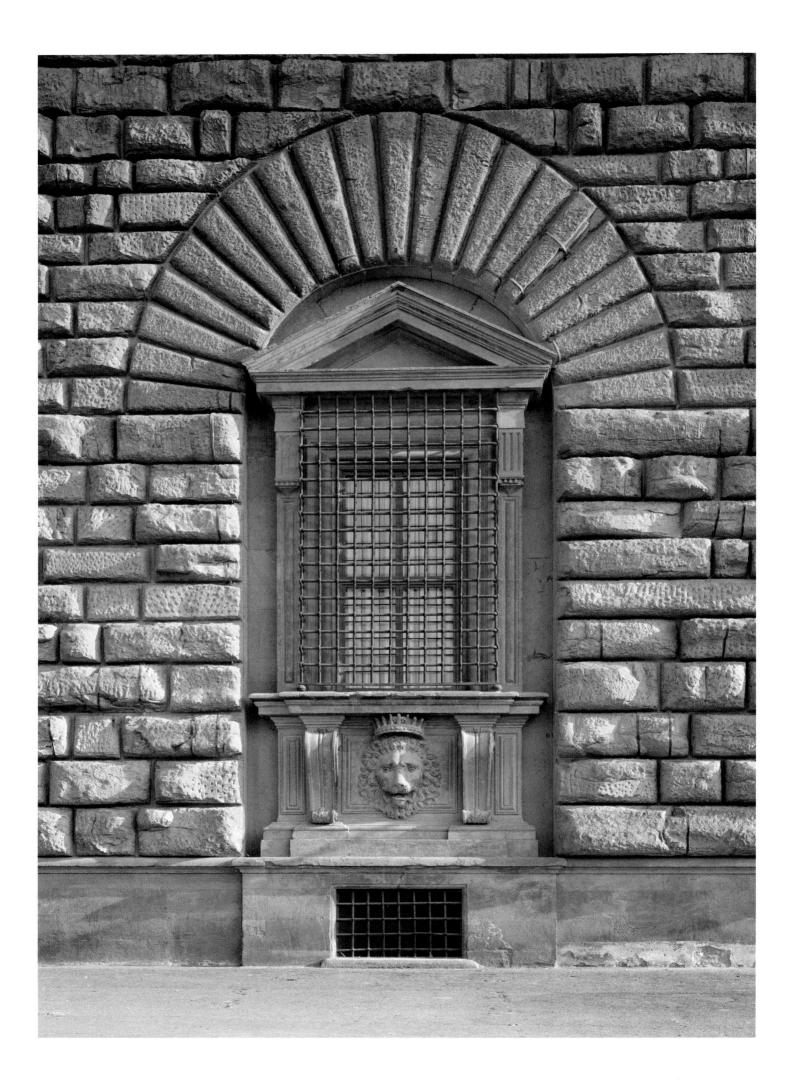

Santa Maria Novella: Ghirlandaio - The Visitation. Three young men in typical fifteenth-century costume lean over a balustrade overlooking the city. The Florence which can be seen in this detail is only in part the real city. On the right, Arnolfo's tower can be seen as it still looks today. On the left, is the top of an idealized turret, over which a flag is waving. The vast cycle of frescoes in the great chapel of Santa Maria Novella was painted by Domenico Ghirlandaio between 1485 and 1490. The Florentine artist was assisted by his brothers, Davide and Benedetto, his brother-in-law, Sebastiano Mainardo, and by other pupils, including a young Michelangelo.

From the Belvedere hill, dominated by the Medici fortress built by Grand Duke Cosimo in 1590, the imposing ramparts completed in the sixteenth century as a defensive network for the city stretch down to the gate at San Niccolò. Their natural setting, even today, is beyond compare, especially in springtime. The centre of Florence with its towers, churches and the colourful profusion of roof-tops lies shimmering dream-like beyond the walls.

The Cathedral (Santa Maria del Fiore) and Palazzo Vecchio by night. Enchanting images like this conjure up another aspect of the city, illuminating its landmarks in carefully studied perspectives. The domes, towers, and the outline of the buildings are of an almost magical quality.

Florence, the Uffizi, with the copy of Michelangelo's David in the foreground (the original is in the Gallery of the Academy). The **Palazzo degli Uffizi** was built by Vasari in the sixteenth century for Cosimo I and houses one of the most important museums in the world. It would take many days to see everything exhibited, including works by Cimabue, Masaccio, Botticelli, Signorelli, Perugino, Dürer, Cranach, Giovanni Bellini, Giorgione and Correggio as well as Michelangelo, Parmigianino, Paolo Veronese, Tintoretto, Caravaggio, Rubens and Rembrandt.

Uffizi Gallery - Tribune. The Florentine architect, Bernardo Buontalenti, built the original structure in the Mannerist period between 1585 and 1589. It has an octagonal plan and a small cupola, decorated with mother-of-pearl shells, by the Florentine Bernardino Barbatelli, known as Poccetti (1548-1612). In the past, it has housed the most important works of art in the Medici collection and today offers a series of sixteenth-century portraits, mainly of members of the Medici family, and other works from the same period. Of these, particularly worthy of mention is the "Medici Venus", a fourth-century copy of a Hellenistic statue found at Hadrian's Villa at Tivoli (Rome) in 1680.

Uffizi Gallery - Second Gallery. This houses the Medici collection of sarcophagi and ancient sculpture. The "Spinario" (Boy Plucking a Thorn from his Foot), a Roman copy of a Greek bronze from the second or first century BC, now in the Palazzo dei Conservatori at Rome, is outstanding. The second-century sarcophagus depicting the "Fall of Phaethon" and the "Seated Girl Preparing to Dance" is also important. Huge windows illuminate the discreet sophistication of the Gallery and its stupendous sixteenth-century ceiling, allowing us a panoramic view over the Arno and the hills.

Uffizi Gallery: Michelangelo - The Doni Tondo. Restored in 1985, the Tondo is one of the most famous paintings in the Gallery. Its colours have now re-emerged in all their cold brilliance to establish the painting as one of the most important and irresistible works of the sixteenth century. The unique, disturbing spiral evolution represents a Holy Family but it is not merely the cold light, absent in other works from this period, which makes the Doni Tondo, and its sumptuous contemporary frame, a unique work of art, for the painting's icono-gaphy is also unusual. Naked, athletic figures inspired by Hellenistic art can be made out in the background beyond the wall while in the foreground on the right is a small St. John the Baptist. The work was commissioned by Agnolo Doni on his marriage to Maddalena Strozzi (1504) or, more likely, in 1507 on the occasion of the birth of their first child, to which the complex symbolism of the painting is said to allude.

Uffizi Gallery: Botticelli - The Birth of Venus (Detail). Dating from around 1485, this most famous of tempera on canvas works depicts Venus "Anadyomene", that is to say, "emerging from the waves". The goddess is being borne to shore on a shell by the wind. On the beach, another goddess, probably Flora, is waiting to clothe her in a robe of royal purple. The work is not a pagan celebration of female beauty but rather has the neo-Platonic significance, characteristic of the Florence of the time, of ideal, spiritual beauty. It combines the classical myth of the birth of Venus from the sea with the Christian concept of the birth of the soul from the waters of baptism. Venus' nudity is therefore symbolic of simplicity and purity.

Uffizi Gallery: Botticelli - Spring. This instantly recognizable painting is said to have been executed for Lorenzo de' Medici, a relative of Lorenzo the Magnificent, who kept it in the villa he acquired at Castello in 1477. The work is joyful and perhaps refers to some happy event of which we are now unaware. Nature's rebirth through love is a neo-Platonic symbol. Zephyr, the wind which brings fertility to Nature, is pursuing Flora. Spring, scattering flowers as she goes, is the issue of their union. In the centre of the painting, we see Venus, the goddess of love, with the blindfolded archer, Eros, overhead. On the left, the three Graces dance in step with their fingers intertwined while Mercury drives the clouds away with his "caduceus" (wand), the symbol of prosperity and peace. There are many complex allegorical levels to this work, not all as yet clarified, but **Spring** remains one of the most celebrated works of the Renaissance for the pure beauty of the figures and the astonishingly realistic variety of flowers depicted in the meadow.

Palazzo Vecchio (or della Signoria): Detail. The exterior of the building is decorated with two rows of marble mullioned trefoil windows set in solid round arches and an imposing dwarf gallery supported by corbels and arches. Under the latter, the sequence of the nine coats of arms of the city is repeated in fresco. The earliest part of the building was built between 1219 and 1314, apparently by Arnolfo di Cambio, as the seat of the Priors (Masters of the Guilds). It was to have been erected where the Uberti family's tower had stood but, when that family's faction fell into disgrace, it was not held right that a public palazzo should be built on "accursed" ground.

Lungarno delle Grazie and Palazzo Vecchio. The symbolic value of the splendid tower (1310) is enhanced by the colours of the evening. It is 94 metres (about 300 feet) high and is built on the base of the older Foraboschi tower, called Torre della Vacca (the Cow Tower). The dwarf gallery is similar to the one on the palazzo, with one or two ornamental variations. The bronze spire (1453) ends in a fleur-de-lis pole with a lion rampant, the city's emblems. According to Lapo da Castiglionchio, Florence had about one hundred and fifty "private" towers in the middle of the fourteenth century, not counting the towers on the city walls. By the end of the century, less than half of these remained.

Loggia della Signoria. Popularly known as the "Loggia dei Lanzi", after the garrison of Landsknechts, notorious Swiss soldiers of fortune hired by Cosimo I de' Medici. It is also called the "Orcagna" loggia from the nickname of Jacopo di Cione, the Florentine artist to whom tradition attributes the design of the late fourteenth-century edifice. The loggia is one of the most significant examples of Florentine Gothic, erected for the investiture of the Priors and other public ceremonies. Of the three slender front arches, the one on the left contains Benvenuto Cellini's famous "Bronze Perseus" (1545-1554) while the group dating from 1583 by the Frenchman, Jean Boulogne, known as Giambologna, the "Rape of the Sabine Women", is on the right.

Piazza della Signoria: Fountain of Neptune. This monumentally eye-catching work (1563-1575) is by Bartolomeo Ammannati and his collaborators, including Giambologna. Ammannati also designed the marvellous courtyard of Palazzo Pitti but the citizens of Florence, who called the white statue of the sea-god, "il Biancone" (the Great White Statue), were not well-disposed towards him and jeered, "Ammannati, Ammannati, what a waste of marble!".

Opera del Duomo Museum: Panels by Luca della Robbia. These panels decorated the base of Giotto's bell-tower together with three others by the same artist and bas-reliefs by Andrea Pisano and his school. They represent Grammar and Arithmetic. Since they were removed in the late Sixties as a precautionary measure, there have been copies on the bell-tower. Giotto himself seems to have inspired some of Pisano's panels. The panels are laid out in two areas and together make up a complete cycle, the first area depicting the life of man as expressed through the arts and sciences while the second shows the planets, the virtues, the liberal arts and the sacraments as they influence that life.

Cathedral (Santa Maria del Fiore) and Giotto's Bell-Tower. Work on the building of the church began on 8th September, 1296, under the architect and sculptor, Arnolfo di Cambio, who also built the original facade, which was very different from the present one. The marvellously harmonious dome was sealed in 1436. The Florentine architect, Filippo Brunelleschi, proposed raising the dome without reinforcement and invented a new herring-bone technique to do so. His structure features a spatially defined and rationally imposed volume which constituted the architectural revolution of the century. The splendid bell-tower named after the great artist is considered by many to be the finest **campanile** in Italy. It is a classic example of Florentine Gothic, built to a square plan, and has 416 steps up to the top of its 84.75-metre (280 feet)-high bulk. Giotto was joined by Andrea Pisano, Francesco Talenti, Nanni di Bartolo, known as Rosso, Alberto Arnoldi and Luca della Robbia on its construction.

Cathedral (Santa Maria del Fiore) and Giotto's Bell-Tower. The present-day facade of the church is a formally correct but lifeless imitation of the local Gothic style by the Florentine, Emilio de Fabris (1881-1888). The overall impression is one of decorative excess, tempered by the shrewd use of the same facing marble white Carrara, green Prato and red Maremma, for both buildings. Giotto worked on the bell-tower for only three years before his death and his contribution ends at the first cornice. The rest is by his pupil, Andrea da Pontedera, called Pisano (1290/1295-1349) and Francesco Talenti (before 1325-1369). The facing in the same marble as the church gives a more intensely alive chromatic force, as befitted the Maestro. In Giotto's own version, the upper part was to have finished in a tall spire.

Battistero: Ghiberti - Door of Paradise, Fall of Jericho. The second panel from the bottom on the right of the Battistero's most celebrated door, the east door dedicated to St. John the Baptist. Here, too, light suffuses everything as the gold on the surface creates rich reflections of warmth to caress the reliefs and bring to life every surface, smooth or protruding. Lorenzo Ghiberti, who was also awarded the commission for the Battistero's northern door, received high praise from his contemporaries for this work.

Battistero di San Giovanni Battista. This splendid Romanesque (eleventh century) building called "fine St. John's" by Dante, was Florence's cathedral from its construction until 1128, probably as a result of the temporary unavailability of the main church of Santa Reparata, which stood where Santa Maria del Fiore now stands. The rectangular tribune, called the "scarsella" or "purse", dates from 1202. It is faced in white and green marble and boasts three bronze doors of uncommon vigour one of which, the one facing the Cathedral, was called the "Door of Paradise" by Michelangelo. The great artist thought it fine enough to open into Paradise itself. The door is the masterpiece of Lorenzo Ghiberti (1425-1452) and is of rare beauty both as a whole and in detail. Its proportions and relationships, its light and shade, and its minute craftsmanship are all carefully studied and of highly sophisticated subtlety.

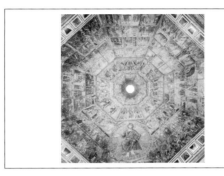

Battistero di San Giovanni Battista: Cupola. The mosaic was executed in the mid-thirteenth century, probably at least in part by Venetian master craftsmen. Mosaics also decorate the vault of the apse (the **scarsella**). The domical vault has, in the cell corresponding to the apse, a huge Christ (over 8 metres, or 25 feet, tall) seated with outstretched arms in a circular cornice. It appears that these mosaics inspired some of the most powerful scenes in Dante's **Inferno.**

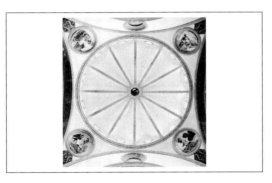

Santa Croce: Cupola of the Pazzi Family Chapel. An original work by Filippo Brunelleschi, this was the last executed by the Florentine architect and was incomplete when he died in 1446. The cupola appears more spacious than it actually is thanks to the effect of the light and the delicate design. It features twelve cells delimited by subtle ribbing, each illuminated by a small circular window. At the edges of the vault are tondoes by Luca della Robbia in glazed earthenware with portraits of the four Evangelists and under these, the same number of crests of the Pazzi family.

Santa Croce and its Surrounding District. The facade of this church, which Italians hold dear for its historical associations, is a nineteenth-century work. It is by Nicolò Matas of Ancona (1853-1863), who was inspired for its design by the chromatic variety of Florentine Gothic. Building began on the church in 1294 but work dragged on well into the fourteenth century. The church was consecrated much later, in 1443. Its ample spaces, majestic solemnity and the careful sobriety of the exterior make it one of the most beautiful Italian Gothic churches. Michelangelo Buonarroti (1475-1564), Vittorio Alfieri (1749-1803), Nicolò Machiavelli (1469-1527), Leonardo da Vinci (1452-1519), Gioacchino Rossini (1792-1868) and Galileo Galilei (1564-1642) are all buried here. The surrounding district was the most insalubrious and poverty-stricken part of the city and was occupied by the Franciscans from the thirteenth century on.

San Lorenzo, New Sacresty: Michelangelo - Tomb of Giuliano de' Medici. On the sarcophagus of Lorenzo the Magnificent's third child, the Duke of Nemours (1487-1516), depicted as a watchful **condottiero,** lie Day (incomplete) and Night, images of Time, whose progress is suggested by the twisting bodies. It is a feature of the New Sacresty (1524-1534) that this funerary monument in the wall is an integral part of the architecture. The surfaces of the block of marble used for the monument are flush with the lines of the structure. The point of focus is in the middle of the sacresty so that the observer becomes an integral part of the space towards which the sculptures seem to be reaching out. Architecture and sculpture work together in complete harmony.

San Lorenzo, New Sacresty: Michelangelo - Tomb of Lorenzo de' Medici. At the feet of the statue of Lorenzo the Magnificent's grandson, appointed Duke of Urbino in 1516, lie Dusk and Dawn, symbols of the ephemeral nature of human life, like Day and Night on the tomb of Giuliano de' Medici. Taken together, the four sculptures express the pointlessness of action. Dawn awakens frowning lazily, Dusk turns away from us, Night sleeps a deep, liberating sleep and Day sits back cross-legged with his chin resting on one shoulder. It is generally agreed that the pessimism Michelangelo left behind in the New Sacresty hides the artist's bitterness at the failure of his youthful ideals. Time had given these the lie and the artist himself was nearing death, as he reveals in his verses.

San Lorenzo's: The Cloister. A Renaissance structure in a clearly Brunelleschian style, its harmonious arches rising over slender pillars with Ionic capitals. The cloister is decorated at regular intervals with marble tondoes featuring the crests of its Medici patrons. The cloister leads to the Medici-Laurentian Library, a sublime piece of architectural genius by Michelangelo (1524), which houses the stupendous collection of Cosimo the Elder later enlarged by Lorenzo the Magnificent.

Santa Maria Novella. The beautiful, intricate facade combines the Romanesque (the small, blind arcades with two-coloured background and corner pillars) and Gothic elements (lancet arches) of the lower part with elements of the Tuscan Renaissance higher up. This blend is the achievement of Leon Battista Alberti, whom the Rucellais commissioned in the mid-fifteenth century to complete the work begun in the early years of the previous century. The architect made a sharp distinction between the older part and the new, to be erected with a double cornice featuring inlaid geometric patterns inspired by Florentine Romanesque, especially that of the church of San Miniato. In the upper part, Alberti disguised the height of the nave with a regular rectangular body featuring four slightly protruding pilaster strips, the whole surmounted by a richly inlaid pediment. Under this, a classical-style inscription commemorates the patron and the date of completion of the work (1470). Two great, finely inlaid scrolls join the top of the nave to those of the aisles.

Santa Maria Novella, Spanish Chapel: Andrea Bonaiuti - The Triumph of the Dominican Church. These frescoes (c. 1355) by the Florentine artist, Andrea Bonaiuti, inspired by the "Mirror of True Penitence" by Jacopo Passavanti (c. 1298-1357), comprise one of the most important cycles of paintings in fourteenth-century Florence and depict the Dominican Order as a new way to salvation. At the bottom, set against a cathedral which is recognizably the original design of the dome of Santa Maria del Fiore, the Great and the Good of this Earth are lined up as the Christian flock gathered at their feet looks on, watched over by black and white sheepdogs (the Dominicans, or "Domini canes", "hounds of the Lord", wore a white robe with a black mantle). The dogs are tearing to pieces the wolves, that is to say the heretics, refuted by St. Dominic, St. Thomas Aquinas and St. Peter the Martyr. The upper scene is of carefree people enjoying themselves as they might in a new earthly Paradise while a Dominican friar absolves a sinner and St. Dominic shows the way to Paradise. St. Peter and two angels stand guard at the gate of Paradise, beyond which the elect joyfully contemplate Christ.

Florence, the Lungarno Avenues from Piazzale Michelangelo. Of course, the sunset adds to the charm of this particular view of the city, but the enchantment of Florence, its walls steeped in history and crossed by a stunningly beautiful river of legendary renown, rises above such fleeting effects. Florence, together with Rome and Venice, is the major city of the arts in Italy. Our photograph makes this point, as a single glance takes in Ponte Vecchio bridge, the Palazzo degli Uffizi and Santa Maria del Fiore.

There is such a concentration of fine arts in Florence that some psychologists have proposed the theory that a surfeit of beauty can occasion a form of malaise. This, according to the as yet untested theory, is supposed to manifest itself as a state of confusion with a loss of identity which scientists have christened "Stendhal's syndrome", after the "crisis of nerves" the French writer suffered on 22nd January, 1817 when he was visiting the funerary monuments in the church of the Santa Croce.

Ponte Vecchio Bridge. The oldest and most famous bridge over the Arno in Florence, crossing the river at its narrowest point. Its origins may be Roman and it has been rebuilt many times. Tradition has it that Neri di Fioravante built a stone bridge here in 1345. German troops gravely damaged the Ponte Vecchio in 1944 and flooding on 4th November, 1966 caused further damage. The bridge, which has three spans, features a series of goldsmiths' and jewellers' shops under the arcade which covers it. Up until the sixteenth century, there were also butchers' shops on it. The double row of shops is interrupted in the middle by terraces which overlook the parapets, offering stunning views.

Ponte Vecchio Bridge: Shops. The goldsmiths' and jewellers' shops are themselves jewels, for they display not only a wide range of jewellery for sale but also many articles of local craftsmanship which, while not for sale, are of great cultural and artisitic interest, such as shelves, shutters, doors and antique locks.

Dome of the Cathedral (Santa Maria del Fiore) and Bell-Tower of the Badia Fiorentina. The two buildings are very different but their perfection of volume and form unites them. We have already spoken about the dome. The bell-tower, on the other hand, is a thrusting, hexagonal construction on a square base attributed to Arnolfo di Cambio. It features four rows of mullion windows from the fourteenth century, the first two Romanesque and the others Gothic, and a pointed spire rising up over a cornice with a double row of arches which crown the whole of the upper central part of the tower.

Santa Maddalena de' Pazzi: Perugino - The Crucifixion. This famous fresco decorates an entire wall of the monastery chapterhouse and dates from 1493-1496. The composition is arranged like a triptych in the three great arches which divide up the wall. The figures are distributed equally, the ones in the two outside groups (St. Bernard and Mary, St. John the Evangelist and St. Benedict) also being posed symmetrically. Christ crucified occupies the centre of the composition with Mary Magdalene kneeling at His feet. The background is the peaceful, rather melancholic, Umbrian countryside. The artist's main strength is his dominance of atmosphere and space, into which he inserts his figures with a poet's sensibility.

Museum of San Marco: Beato Angelico - The Last Judgement. The strongly religious and mystic spirit of Beato Angelico is evident

in the detail of the great work, dating from around 1430, with its saints and high-ranking prelates. The artist was the first at the beginning of the fifteenth century to learn Masaccio's lesson and imbue his paintings with realism and a sense of perspective.

San Marco: Monk's Cell. Fra' Giovanni da Fiesole, better known as Beato Angelico, painted cells and corridors in this Dominican monastery, which Michelozzo had rebuilt between 1439 and 1450. There is no drama in the compositions and even the most sorrowful subjects, such as the Crucifixion, are contemplated with that serenity which springs from a knowledge that everything that happens is God's will and serves His purpose. Beato Angelico's work is spiritual and plainly didactic but it also skilfully incorporates the clarity with which the Florentine Renaissance depicted the human figure and inanimate objects.

Galleria dell'Accademia: Michelangelo - Prison. The statue reproduced here is the most famous of the four great statues called "prisons", or "slaves", which Michelangelo sculpted for the tomb Pope Julius II planned (and only partially built) in St. Peter's in Rome. The four have an awe-inspiring dramatic atmosphere expressed through the subject and through their unfinished state, which underlines the contrast between form and "non-form", the ideal and the concrete, life and death. They were probably executed between 1530 and 1534, when the artist was most inward-looking and meditating most pessimistically on the human condition.

Galleria dell'Accademia: Michelangelo - David. This 4.10-metre (13 feet) tall statue is symbolic of the Florentine republic fighting tyrants in the name of Liberty. The artist chose to represent not action, but the moral impulse and internal tension immediately preceding action. As our gaze moves up the statue, the pathos becomes more intense, the inclined leg initiating a series of precise movements which includes the sharp flexing of the wrist, the unexpected movement of the head and the arm bending back towards the shoulder. David is huge because physical size here also stands for moral stature. He is naked because his only weapon is his own virtue. The anatomical details in the veins of the hand resting on the thigh and the muscles on the neck highlight differences in tension in different parts of the body.

Museo Nazionale del Bargello: Donatello - David. An early work by the great, and prolific, Florentine sculptor, who worked on until his death at an advanced age. This statue portrays the legendary Biblical hero, a subject Donatello was to tackle again in bronze (the work is on exhibition in the same hall of the museum). The structure of this marble piece clearly evinces the heritage of the late fourteenth century in both the outline and in the dynamic torsion of the trunk.

Museo Nazionale del Bargello: Jean Boulogne, called Giambologna - Various Sculptures. The loggia on the first floor of this splendid palazzo, formerly seat of the **Bargello,**

or Captain of Justice, and a notorious place of imprisonment and torture from the fifteenth to the eighteenth centuries, has been a museum since 1859. It houses many bronzes and marbles by the French-born sculptor, Giambologna (1524-1608), among which are a goshawk, an eagle, a peacock, several **puttos** or small boys and a celebrated Mercury (dating from 1564) in a stupendous running pose, the body strained and tense, with a wealth of exquisite detail.

Palazzo Pitti: Ammannati's Courtyard and the Artichoke Fountain. Bartolomeo Ammannati laboured on the transformation of the rear part of Palazzo Pitti between 1558 and 1570 on the instructions of Cosimo I de' Medici. The great porticoed courtyard echoes the fifteenth-century palazzo's facade, with the enormous blocks of rough-cut stone (called "rustic ashlar") and the keystones of the arches decorated with masks and ram's heads, for Aries was one of Cosimo's emblems. The palazzo was transformed into a suburban palace and became the official seat of the Medici dynasty, now of Grand Ducal rank. In 1621, on the death of Cosimo II, last of the dynasty, the Lorenas took over the palazzo as did the House of Savoy after the Unification of Italy. The Artichoke Fountain, with its lively octagonal basin, is by Francesco Ferrucci, known as Francesco del Tadda, from Fiesole (1497-1585). The obelisk and the priceless ancient basin on the first great terrace of the Boboli Gardens (amphitheatre) are, respectively, from Egypt and the Thermal Baths of Caracalla in Rome.

Palazzo Pitti, Palatine Gallery: The Jupiter Room and Raffaello - The Veiled Woman. The beautiful, anonymous young woman, thought by some to be the legendary **Fornarina** or "baker's girl" with whom Raffaello was in love, is wearing rich clothes and precious jewelry, which denote aristocratic origins. The usual backgound scenery is missing, so the observer can concentrate on the subject's psychological aspect. The sober colours of the Veiled Woman highlight the warmth of her gaze and the delicate vitality of her complexion. The elaborate, leg-of-mutton sleeve is typical of the fashion of the period.

Florence, Boboli Gardens: The Painted Grotto. "The Boboli Gardens are not large – you wonder how compact little Florence finds room for them within her walls," said Henry James. He added, "But they are scattered to their extreme, their all romantic advantage and felicity, over steep undulations between the rugged and terraced palace and a still-surviving stretch of city wall, where the unevenness of the ground much adds to their apparent size." The Boboli were laid out by Tribolo, an expert landscape gardener, and provide a verdant breathing-space away from the city's bustle.

Panorama. The dome of Santa Maria del Fiore is a well-known observation point. The view crystallizes Florence's uniqueness as a town, its geographical setting, its shapes and its colours offering a panorama of the city from Palazzo Bargello to Palazzo Pitti, with the Badia Fiorentina, Palazzo Vecchio, the Loggia della Signoria and the church of Orsanmichele. Behind Palazzo Pitti can be seen the Boboli Gardens and the Belvedere hill with the Belvedere on top.

Palazzo Pitti: Detail. The spectacular facade of this imposing palazzo is one of the best examples of **bugnato,** or ashlarwork, a wall facing of hewn masonry blocks. The term "bugna" refers to the projecting part of the hewn blocks, called "bunia" in the tongue of the Gauls and meaning a "bulging tree trunk". The fine windows on the ground floor are all decorated with a triangular tympanum, or gable, and a small parapet between the supports of which is a high-relief crowned lion's head, one of the emblems of Florence.

Palazzo Medici-Riccardi. A typical Florentine Renaissance palazzo with its majestic, elegant facade where the power of the lower ashlarwork is attenuated higher up. It features the double sequence of slender round arch mullion windows and an elegant classical cornice on brackets under the roof. Cosimo I de' Medici preferred the more secure Palazzo Vecchio to this, the original Medici family residence, built between 1444 and 1460 and home to the Elder Cosimo, Lorenzo the Magnificent and Caterina de' Medici, later Queen of France. All the works of art and stupendous ornaments were transferred to the new palace and from there, to Palazzo Pitti and the Uffizi. The palazzo passed to the Riccardis in 1659 when the Marquis Gabriello and Senator Francesco Riccardi acquired it and immediately set about extending and renovating it.

Palazzo Medici-Riccardi: First Courtyard. The area is marked out by a classical portico surmounted by a row of mullion windows similar to those on the facade and by an Ionic colonnade. The mullion windows rest on a sort of great architrave decorated with medallions and festoons, the former attributed to the Florentine, Bertoldo di Giovanni (1420-1491) and the latter to Maso di Bartolomeo from Arezzo (1406-1456). Under the portico, we find Roman remains, sculptures in rich settings and a classical-style marble statue of Orpheus mounted on a monumental pedestal decorated with Medici emblems, eagles and lion's heads, by the Florentine, Baccio Bandinelli (1488-1560).

Palazzo of the Wool Guild and Church of Orsanmichele: Details. The Gothic corner shrine of the ancient palazzo, with its suspended porch delimited by two spiral pillars, guards an early fourteenth-century Coronation of the Virgin by Jacopo Landini, known as "il Casentino". The architecture blends perfectly with that of the church next door, a striking monument with imposing thirteenth-century arches closed off by wide Gothic three-light windows decorated with tracery and flanked by shrines which contain statues. Before its consecration in 1380, the building, dating from 1290, was a grain market.

Hill of San Miniato. The hill has to offer, as well as the church, the massive, crenellated Palazzo dei Vescovi with its elegant, fourteenth-century mullion windows. The building was originally the bishop's summer residence, then a barracks, a convent, a hospital for infectious diseases, a Jesuit college and, finally, the Olivetan monastery it is today. The Fort improvised by Michelangelo when Imperial troops laid siege to Florence in 1530 remains as does the unfinished sixteenth-century bell-tower, also used by the artist during the 1530 siege and still bearing the scars left by Spanish cannonballs. The church is the most important example of Florentine Romanesque. Like the Battistero, it is faced in white and green marble in series of five arches with alternate real and false portals, the latter being blind. The upper part corresponds to the height of the nave and has a finely sculpted twelfth-century classical-style window in the middle. This is surrounded by a thirteenth-century mosaic depicting Christ in the act of benediction enthroned between the Virgin and St. Miniato, the first Florentine martyr.

San Miniato al Monte. A jewel of Florentine Romanesque, the church dates back to the eleventh and twelfth centuries. Its scenic location and the elegant green and white marble facade make it one of Florence's most admired landmarks. Inside, there are works by Michelozzo, Luca della Robbia, Spinello Aretino and Alesso Baldovinetti.

San Miniato: Interior. The church features a nave flanked by two aisles with a richly inlaid marble floor (1207) where the signs of the zodiac, lions and doves can be made out, amongst other emblems. In front of the crypt, Michelozzo's delicate Renaissance chapel (1442) is decorated with terracotta coffers by Luca della Robbia (1448). It was constructed for the Crucifix of St. Giovanni Gualberto, founder of the Vallombrosa Benedictine congregation. The raised presbytery, closed off by an elegant balustrade with marble rosettes inlaid in a delicate pulpit, boasts a richly decorated bowl with a thirteenth-century mosaic on the same subject as that on the upper part of the facade. St. Miniato appears, crown in hand, denoting his imperial origins.

Medici Villa at Artimino, known as "La Fernanda". One of the Medici family's most important country residences, this villa is also called the villa of a hundred chimneys, and a glance at the roof shows why. It was built in the sixteenth century, at the height of the Grand Ducal court's splendour.

Villa La Pietra: The Rotunda. This typical aristocratic villa in the hills has been for a long time the residence of one of Florence's most refined admirers, the Englishman, Sir Harold Acton. Sir Harold is the author of many volumes on the history and art of his adopted city and is also a discriminating collector of antiquities. The villa features a splendid garden, still kept according to the canons of the classic Italian garden. The hedges are trimmed carefully by skilled gardeners into precise geometrical, and even animal, shapes.

Medici Villa at Poggio a Caiano, Main Hall: Frescoes with Roman Subjects. This superb Medici villa is a masterpiece by Giuliano da Sangallo, who designed it at the behest of Lorenzo the Magnificent (c. 1480). Its internal decoration was completed over a century later. Filippino Lippi began the frescoes in the entrance hall in 1492. Pontormo the worked on those in the main hall, followed by Franciabigio and Andrea del Sarto. Allori only finished the work about 1582. The iconographic scheme glorifying the Medicis was drawn up by the learned Paolo Giovio, who related episodes in the Medici family history to the stories of ancient Rome.

Garden of the Medici Villa at Castello. A few miles from the centre of Florence on the outskirts of the city lies this old Medici villa, which was reconstructed in the sixteenth century for the Grand Dukes by Bartolomeo Ammannati. The garden is laid out in the classic Italian style with fountains, grottoes and magnificent lemon-trees. Today, the villa is the home of the prestigious **Accademia della Crusca,** a learned institution dedicated to the study of the Italian language.

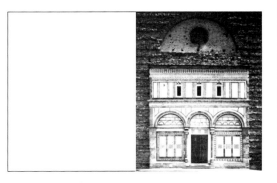

San Domenico di Fiesole, Badia Fiesolana: Detail. This great, austere place of worship was the cathedral of Fiesole in the Florentine hills until 1206. It was rebuilt for the first time in the thirteenth century by the Camaldolites and again in the fifteenth century, thanks to the generosity of Cosimo the Elder, by the Augustinian Canons Regular, or Laterans, of the Congragation of St. Frediano. The Laterans were known as the **Roccettini,** or "Bobbin-Monks", after their traditional implement. The front of the church is incomplete and incorporates part of the facade of the earlier Romanesque building whose green and white marble brings to mind the facing of the Battistero in Florence and the basilica of San Miniato.